westermann

Six Friends
at Caxton Castle

PAMELA HANUS

W0087102

5

Passend zum Lehrwerk:
Camden Town
Textbook 5
(ISBN 978-3-14-149220-0)

© 2020 Bildungshaus Schulbuchverlage
Westermann Schroedel Diesterweg Schöningh Winklers GmbH,
Georg-Westermann-Allee 66, 38104 Braunschweig
www.westermann.de

Druck A⁴ / Jahr 2024
Alle Drucke der Serie A sind im Unterricht parallel verwendbar.

Redaktion: Tanja Mees
Illustrationen: Ulf Marckwort
Umschlaggestaltung: LIO Design GmbH, Braunschweig
Layout: LIO Design GmbH, Braunschweig; thom bahr GRAFIK, Mainz
Druck und Bindung: Westermann Druck GmbH,
Georg-Westermann-Allee 66, 38104 Braunschweig

ISBN 978-3-14-**149337**-5

Contents

Characters

Narrator
Emma
Caroline
Charlie
George
Gillian
Rajiv
Tom, thief
Dave, thief
Guard 1, Sid
Guard 2, Bert
Guard 3
Guard 4
Policeman 1, Bill
Policeman 2, Harry

Scene 1: On the train

The children are sitting on chairs. It looks like they are on a train.

Narrator: The children are on a train. They are very excited because they are going to Caxton Castle.

5 **Emma:** Isn't this great? Here we are together on a train to Caxton Castle. I'm so excited!

Caroline: Mmh! I love days out, especially if I have a delicious picnic.

Gillian: And I love castles. They're fun places.

10 **Emma:** I think so, too. And we can find out about people's lives hundreds of years ago. There's an audio guide and some fantastic historical things to see – it says so on the website.

George: I'm not interested in boring old history! The best
15   thing about this day out is that we can do what we like all day – yippee! No parents to tell us what to look at and where to go.

(speaks like George's mother) Come here, George, and look at this famous picture. You really should be more
20   interested in history, you know – life isn't all about football!

The children laugh.

---

scene /siːn/ – *Szene*   train /treɪn/ – *Zug* **3** narrator /nəˈreɪtə/ – *Erzähler*
4 castle /ˈkɑːs(ə)l/ – *Schloss; Burg* **7** day out /deɪˈaʊt/ – *Tagesausflug* **11** ago
/əˈɡəʊ/ – *vor* **14** to be interested in /ˌbiˈɪntrəstɪd ɪn/ – *sich interessieren (für)*

4

Caroline: Well, there's lots of history at Caxton Castle, George!

George: Yeah! But there are lots more fun things to see – like jousting, with knights on horses.

George and Charlie act like knights. They ride horses and
5 *point their arms. They try to knock each other back in their*
seats. Rajiv plays the game, too.

Rajiv: Well, that should be fun. Can we take part in the jousting, too?

3 jousting /ˈdʒaʊstɪŋ/ – *Lanzenstechen* **3** knight /naɪt/ – *Ritter* **5** to knock /nɒk/ – *stoßen* **5** each other /ˌiːtʃˈʌðə/ – *gegenseitig*

Scene 1: On the train

Charlie: No, we just watch it – if we want to.

Rajiv: That's boring. I want to be a real knight.

Charlie: Ha! Rajiv, that's just the thing for you. Don't worry, you can be a knight anyway and fight the ghost of Caxton Castle.

Emma: *(excited)* Ghost! A real ghost?

Charlie: They say that you can see the ghost of Sir Percival Caxton in the castle every night at 12 o'clock.

Charlie stands up and walks like a ghost.

---

4 to fight /faɪt/ – *kämpfen* **4** ghost /gəʊst/ – *Geist*

Caroline: *(angry)* Sit down, Charlie! Don't listen to him, Emma – it's not true.

Charlie: It is! It's on the website. Just think – a real ghost! I really want to meet him.

5 **Gillian:** And why does he haunt the castle? There must be a reason.

Charlie: *(speaks like a ghost)* They say he cannot sleep because he is looking for his murderer.

Emma: *(excited)* A real murderer!

10 **Gillian:** Don't get too excited, Emma. I'm sure he isn't there anymore.

Charlie: *(laughing)* Anyway, the ghost comes out at night and our train home leaves at 5:30.

Announcement: Next stop – Woodend Station. Leave the
15 train here for Caxton Castle. Please take all your things with you. We hope you have a nice day.

Rajiv: Come on everybody. Stop talking about ghosts and murderers. It's time to get out.

---

5 to haunt /hɔːnt/ – *heimsuchen* **8** murderer /ˈmɜː(r)dərə(r)/ – *Mörder*
11 anymore /ˌeniˈmɔː/ – *nicht mehr* **14** announcement /əˈnaʊnsmənt/ – *Ansage* **18** to get out /ˌgetˈaʊt/ – *aussteigen*

The children show their tickets and walk by some small tents.
People are calling out 'Popcorn! Hot dogs! Lovely presents to
take home!'

Narrator: The children come to the castle and see lots of
small tents with food and drink in front of the castle.
They can hear people cheering at the jousting.

Gillian: Mmm! Those hot dogs look good!

Emma: They do, but it's so warm – I'd love to have an ice
cream. Can you see a sign for ice cream, Caroline?

---

grounds /graʊndz/ – *Gelände* **1** to walk by /ˌwɔːk ˈbaɪ/ – *vorbeigehen an*
1 tent /tent/ – *Zelt*

Caroline: Look! I think there's one over there. But why don't we wait for a bit? We've got a fantastic picnic lunch.

Gillian: That's a good idea.

George: I don't believe it! Here we are at a castle with jousting
5   and ghosts and all you lot can think about is food. Come on, Rajiv and Charlie. The jousting is over there behind those people. Let's go!

Rajiv: Well, actually I'm quite hungry and I'd like something to eat first.

10 **George:** *(angry)* Oh, really! Come on, Charlie! There are so many exciting things here – food is not important.

George gallops away like a horse. Charlie laughs and follows him.

Gillian: Look, there's some grass over there. Let's sit down.

The children sit down and begin to eat their lunches.

15 **Caroline:** Who wants one of my cheese sandwiches? What have you got, Emma?

Emma: Chicken nuggets! Mmm. My favourite.

Gillian: Can I have a chicken nugget and give you a piece of cake?

20 **Emma:** OK! Here you are.

---

8 actually /ˈæktʃuəli/ – *wirklich* **8** I'd like ... (= I would like ...) /ˌaɪd ˈlaɪk/ – *Ich hätte gern ...* **12** to follow /ˈfɒləʊ/ – *folgen*

Scene 2: In the castle grounds

Caroline: What about me? Can I have a chicken nugget, too?

Suddenly Rajiv sees two men hiding behind a hot dog tent.
Their clothes are black and one has got a sack. One of them
puts a mask over his face. The other one takes it away from
5 *him and is very angry. He looks around to see if anybody can*
see them. The two men are arguing.

Rajiv: Listen, everybody. Don't look now, but those two men
over there are behaving in a very strange way.

Caroline: How can we see their strange behaviour if we can't
10 look at them, Rajiv?

---

4 mask /mɑːsk/ – *Maske* **6** to argue /ˈɑːgjuː/ – *sich streiten*

Rajiv: Well, don't all look at once! One of them has got a mask. I can hide behind them and see what I can find out.

Caroline: I'm sure they are just part of the show.

Gillian: But they look a bit strange. Let me come with you,
5   Rajiv.

Rajiv: No, you stay here – they may leave if we all go there.

Rajiv goes to the two men in black who are hiding behind a tent. They can't see him. He listens to their conversation. Tom and Dave are not very clever – and Dave is easily scared.

10 **Tom:** Listen, Dave. It's very easy. We go into the castle and hide there. When it closes, we have lots of time to take the silver and the jewellery. Then we climb out of a window and go to the car. Nobody gets hurt. With the money we can buy a ticket to America.

15 **Dave:** *(worried)* But what if they catch us? Then it's not America but prison for us. *(very unhappy)* I don't want to go to prison again.

Tom: Don't be such a baby. I'm a very clever person and it's a very clever plan. Nothing can go wrong this time.

20 **Dave:** But you always say that, Tom, and something always goes wrong.

---

1 at once /ət ˈwʌns/ – *gleichzeitig* **8** conversation /ˌkɒnvəˈseɪʃ(ə)n/ – *Unterhaltung* **12** silver /ˈsɪlvə/ – *Silber* **12** jewellery /ˈdʒuːəlri/ – *Schmuck* **13** Nobody gets hurt. – *Niemand wird verletzt.* **15** to catch /kætʃ/ – *einfangen* **17** prison /ˈprɪz(ə)n/ – *Gefängnis* **19** to go wrong /ˌɡəʊ ˈrɒŋ/ – *schiefgehen*

Scene 2: In the castle grounds

Tom: Just shut up and follow me. I know what I'm doing! And
put that mask in the sack before we go into the castle.

*Dave puts the mask in the sack. Tom puts the sack under his
jumper so that he looks fat. Then he walks away, Dave follows*
5 *him. Rajiv waits for them to leave and runs back to the girls.*

Rajiv: Those men are really thieves! They are planning to steal
some silver and jewellery from the castle. What can we
do?

Emma: Come on, let's find a castle guard and tell them. They
10 know what to do.

The children run off the stage.

---

6 thief (*pl* thieves) /θi:f, θi:vz/ – *Dieb* **6** to steal /sti:l/ – *stehlen* **9** guard
/gɑːd/ – *Wärter* **11** off /ˈɒf/ – *hinunter*

Scene 3: Talking to the guards

The guards are drinking tea and talking when the children run towards them. The children are out of breath and find it difficult to speak.

Narrator: The children see two guards. They run to them.
5   They are all shouting at once.

Rajiv: Some men … over there … they want to steal some things …

Emma: Hurry up … in the castle … two thieves …

Caroline: You must catch them … very bad men …

10 **Gillian:** Two men in black … with masks … one with a sack …

The guards don't look very pleased.

Guard 1, Sid: Now, just calm down a minute. Stop talking all at once.

Guard 2, Bert: *(angry)* I'm just having a break. Don't make all
15   this noise.

Emma: *(excited)* It's important. Two men are planning to steal some things from the castle.

Guard 1, Sid: *(angry)* Oh, really! So, how do you know that? Are they your friends?

---

1 tea /tiː/ – *Tee* **2** to be out of breath /ˌbiˌ aʊtˌəv ˈbreθ/ – *außer Atem sein*
8 to hurry up /ˌhʌriˌ ˈʌp/ – *sich beeilen*

Rajiv: Of course they aren't. Listen! They are planning to steal jewellery and silver and then go to America.

Guard 1, Sid: Oh, they've got a plan, have they? Well, we all have plans, don't we? But plans change! At the moment
5   Bert here is planning to have a chocolate biscuit with his tea. But perhaps Bert may decide to have a different one!

Guard 2, Bert: That's right, Sid. Plans change a lot. Now, your thieves may decide to go to Canada and not America. So
10   we look for them in America and they aren't there.

Caroline: *(frustrated)* That's stupid. They mustn't go into the castle!

Guard 1, Sid: Of course they can go in if they've got a ticket!

Rajiv: But they're thieves!

15 **Guard 2, Bert:** So you say. But it's our tea break now. Come back in half an hour and we can talk about it then.

Gillian: Come on, everyone. We need a different plan. Let's go!

Rajiv and the girls go off the stage.

---

11 frustrated /frʌˈstreɪtɪd/ – *frustriert, enttäuscht* **11** stupid /ˈstjuːpɪd/ – *blöd*

George and Charlie are standing on one side of the stage. They are clapping their hands and cheering. The audience cannot see their faces.

Narrator: The children decide to look for George and Charlie
5   and tell them about the thieves.

George: That black knight is really fantastic! The others don't have a chance. He's so strong!

Charlie: What a great fight! But I wouldn't like to fall down in all that armour.

10 *The other children come onto the stage.*

Caroline: *(calls)* George, Charlie! Listen. We need your help!

---

1 side /saɪd/ – *Seite* **8** fight /faɪt/ – *Kampf* **9** armour /ˈɑːmə/ – *Rüstung*
10 onto /ˈɒntə/ – *auf*

George and Charlie look at their friends.

George: I can help you finish your lunch if you like. I'm so hungry after the exciting tournament.

Rajiv: We haven't got time for food now. This is important.

5 **Charlie:** Oh, that's new. Food isn't important anymore! So, what's important now?

Gillian: *(excited)* Two men in black are planning to steal some silver and jewellery from the castle.

George: Wow! How do you know?

10 **Rajiv:** Because they were talking about it behind a hot dog tent.

Emma: *(frustrated)* And the stupid guards don't believe us! They think we are making it all up. They just want their tea break of course!

15 **George:** *(thinks)* Well, let's show the stupid guards that we don't need their help. We can stop the thieves alone.

Gillian: I don't understand, George.

George: There are six of us and only two thieves. I think we can make sure the thieves don't steal the silver and
20 jewellery without the guards. Now, tell me about the men, Rajiv. What are they like?

---

3 tournament /ˈtʊənəmənt/ – *Turnier* **10** were talking about it – *sprachen darüber* **13** to make up /ˌmeɪk ˈʌp/ – *sich ausdenken* **16** to stop /stɒp/ – *aufhalten* **19** to make sure /ˌmeɪk ˈʃɔː/ – *sicherstellen*

Rajiv: Well, one is called Tom and one is called Dave. They are wearing black clothes and Dave has got a mask – but he's not wearing it. … Oh. And Tom has got a sack under his jumper.

5 **George:** Mmh! Should be easy to find them!

Emma: *(nervous)* I think we should ring our parents and tell them about it. We can't catch the thieves alone. It's dangerous. I don't like it.

Gillian: Oh, Emma. George is right – there are more of us.
10 And anyway – it's exciting. What do you think, Rajiv? Are the men dangerous?

Rajiv: Well, it's difficult to believe that they are very dangerous. They seem quite stupid to me. Dave is very nervous and makes mistakes – like wearing his mask
15 when everyone can see him. Tom thinks he's clever but I'm not so sure. I don't think they are dangerous because Tom said: 'Nobody gets hurt.'

George: Well, I think you are right. Come on! Let's all go to the castle now.

20 **Caroline:** Good idea, George. We can tell the guards in the castle about the two men. I'm sure they are better than the guards outside.

George: Perhaps, but my plan is to follow the men in black and find out where they want to hide. When we know
25 that, we can call the police.

---

13 to seem /siːm/ – *scheinen*

Charlie: Sounds like a great plan to me … and lots of fun. We
can follow them around like detectives. I'm Sherlock
and you're John Watson! What about the rest of you?

Charlie walks around the friends, looking over shoulders and
5 *hiding behind them.*

Caroline: It's not really a game, Charlie. These are real thieves
and we are just children.

Emma: Caroline is right. This is too big for us.

Gillian: Oh, come on you two. Let's have some fun! Nothing
10   can happen and we can always tell a guard if we have a
problem.

Scene 4: George's plan

Gillian high fives George and Charlie.

Rajiv: I'm in, too.

Rajiv high fives them, too.

George: Come on then, let's go! What about you two?

5 *Caroline and Emma don't look very happy.*

Caroline: Well, I think I have to stay with my little brother,
   don't I? Come on Emma. Don't look so unhappy.

The children leave.

---

1 to high five /ˌhaɪ ˈfaɪv/ – *sich abklatschen* **2** I'm in. – *Ich bin dabei.*

Scene 5: The Great Hall

The children enter the Great Hall. There are some paintings on the wall, some old furniture, some suits of armour and a long table. There is a long tablecloth and lots of pieces of silver on the table. They look around. There may be other people
5 *walking around.*

Narrator: The children show their tickets and go into the Great Hall of the castle. They talk about how to find the thieves.

George: *(whispers)* OK, everyone, come here and listen to
10 me. I think we should form two groups to look for the thieves.

Charlie: Good thinking, George. What about a boys' group and a girls' group?

Rajiv: We should mix the groups. The girls may get scared
15 alone.

Gillian: *(angry)* Oh really, Rajiv! Not all girls get scared!

Emma: Well, I'm not scared, but I want to be in Caroline's group!

Caroline: That's fine with me, and Rajiv can come with us, too!

20 **George:** *(laughs)* Rajiv, the knight in armour, helper and friend of the young girls in the castle!

---

hall /hɔːl/ – *Halle* **1** to enter /ˈentə/ – *betreten* **1** painting /ˈpeɪntɪŋ/ – *Gemälde*
2 furniture /ˈfɜːnɪtʃə/ – *Möbel* **2** suit of armour /suːt̬_əv̬_ˈɑːmə/ – *Ritterrüstung*
3 tablecloth /ˈteɪb(ə)l‚klɒθ/ – *Tischdecke* **19** That's fine with me. – *Das ist in Ordnung.*

Rajiv: Stop it, George! I'm happy with my group. You OK, Gillian?

Gillian: Why not? Then I can fight Sir Percival when George and Charlie are scared!

5 **Charlie:** Ha, ha. Very funny, Gillian!

George: *(whispers)* Shh! So now we look for Tom and Dave – but they mustn't know what we are doing, so be careful. If one group finds their hiding place, they watch it and text the other group. The other group then call the
10 police and we catch them. What do you think?

Gillian: I think the plan is OK, but we should keep in contact every half an hour in our group chat.

Caroline: Well done, Gillian. That's important. Has everyone got a mobile with them?

15 *They all high five.*

Emma: *(looks at her mobile)* But my signal isn't very good.

George: It's OK. You've got Caroline and Rajiv with you. OK, everyone, let's go!

They leave the stage. Tom and Dave come in from the other
20 *side. They are both wearing masks and Dave is looking scared.*

Dave: I'm not happy, Tom.

---

13 Well done. /ˌwel ˈdʌn/ – *Gut gemacht.* **16** signal /ˈsɪgn(ə)l/ – *Empfang*

Tom: *(angry)* Oh, really, Dave. What's wrong now?

Dave: I've got this funny feeling, Tom!

Tom: What funny feeling, Dave?

Dave: *(scratches his left ear)* My ear itches, Tom. Something
5   is wrong with your plan and it's making me nervous.
When I'm nervous, my right ear always itches. Believe
me, it's a bad sign.

Tom: *(angry)* But you're scratching your left ear, Dave!

Dave: *(surprised)* Oh, am I? Well, my right ear is itching, too.
10   I'm still nervous, Tom, and I don't want to go to prison
again.

4 to scratch /skrætʃ/ – *kratzen* **4** to itch /ɪtʃ/ – *jucken*

Tom: *(puts his hand on Dave's arm)* Don't worry. I know what I'm doing. Now let's find a place to hide. What about under that table over there?

They hear voices.

5   Come on, Dave, hurry up. There's somebody coming!

They hide under the table. Rajiv, Emma and Caroline come in.

Caroline: There are so many places to hide here. How can we find them?

Emma: Look, there's a guard. Why don't we tell him about the
10   two men in black now?

4 voice /vɔɪs/ – *Stimme*

Rajiv: *(whispers)* No, Emma. We can't do that without asking George. Anyway, the guard doesn't look very friendly. Don't say anything, please!

Guard 3: *(unfriendly)* Hey, you three. Why are you standing
5   around here? Move on, now.

Caroline: *(looks at a painting)* We're just looking at this fantastic painting of …, of …

Rajiv: *(reads)* … of Sir Percival Caxton. It … er … it … er … looks … just like him!

10 **Guard 3:** *(unfriendly)* How do you know what he looks like? This painting is three hundred years old.

Emma: *(nervous)* Isn't he the ghost of Caxton Castle? We know a lot about him.

Guard 3: *(pushes the children to the door)* That's right, Miss –
15   and if you stay too long in one place, he may just come and find you. Now, just move along to the next room please!

The children leave, the guard follows them. Tom and Dave
come out from under the table. Dave is really upset and wants
20 *to leave the castle now.*

Dave: See, Tom! Those kids know about us. That's enough for me, I'm leaving.

---

21 kid *(informal)* /kɪd/– Kind

Scene 5: The Great Hall

Tom: *(holds his arm)* But Dave, they're just some silly kids looking for an adventure, that's nothing to worry about. We just have to hide. When the castle closes at 5 o'clock, they must go. Then we are alone. Now, just chill!

5 **Dave:** *(unhappy)* But I'm hungry.

Tom: Shut up and follow me.

---

2 adventure /ədˈventʃə/ – *Abenteuer* **3** We just have to hide. – *Wir müssen uns nur verstecken.* **4** to chill *(informal)* /tʃɪl/ – *sich entspannen*

Gillian, Charlie and George come into the Great Hall. They look around them to see if the guard is coming.

Narrator: Gillian, Charlie and George can't find the thieves and now they don't know where their friends are. A castle guard follows them in every room so that they can't really look for the thieves.

George: That guard is horrible. Why doesn't he go away?

Gillian: He is worried. He thinks we are planning to do something wrong.

Charlie: So, what do we do now?

George: I think we should hide now. When the castle closes for the night, we can look for the men in black.

Gillian: Isn't that a bit dangerous? I mean, they close the doors and then we're alone with the thieves.

Charlie: Come on, Gillian – that's a really exciting idea, George. Perhaps we can see the ghost at 12 o'clock.

Gillian: *(laughs)* I don't think Emma and Caroline really want to see a ghost! But whatever! We must tell the others what the new plan is.

George: OK! When the guard comes, we can run and then meet back here later. Tell the others if you see them.

---

1 to look around /ˌlʊk_əˈraʊnd/ – *sich umsehen* **13** to mean /miːn/ – *meinen*

Scene 6: The hiding place

Gillian: I can send them a text message. We should keep in contact, anyway.

Gillian takes out her mobile phone, but just then the guard comes in.

5   **Guard 4:** *(angry)* Eh, you. No mobile phones in the castle. Give me that, miss!

Gillian: No chance. Come on. Let's go.

The children run different ways and the guard doesn't know what to do.

10   **Guard 4:** *(shouts)* Come here, you horrible kids!

The guard leaves stage right. Rajiv, Emma, Caroline and Gillian come back from stage left. Gillian is telling them about George's plan.

Emma: I'm not interested in what George says. I'm not
5   staying here all night.

Gillian: But we have only got this chance to catch the thieves, Emma.

Caroline: But how do we get out of here later when the doors are closed?

10 **Emma:** And I'm sure it's really dark outside. I want to go home.

George and Charlie come running in from the other side.

George: Hurry up, everyone hide under the table. The guard is coming.

15 *The children hide under the table. The audience can see them but not the guard.*

Guard 4: *(frustrated)* So you think you can play games with me, do you? Well, you don't know me very well, do you? I'm not that stupid!

20 *The guard leaves. Then you hear the following message. The guard is speaking with a microphone.*

---

8 to get out of *(informal)* /ˌget ˈaʊt əv/ – *herauskommen* **9** closed /kləʊzd/ – *geschlossen*

Announcement: All visitors must leave the castle. We are closing now.

The lights go out. There is a small scream from Emma.

George: *(turns his mobile torch on)* Shhhh! Emma.

5 **Caroline:** George! Are you sure this is a good idea? I think it's dangerous.

Rajiv: I think Caroline's right, George. We can't stay here all night.

Charlie: Why not? Then we can catch the thieves and perhaps
10   see a ghost!

Emma: *(gets out her phone)* Why don't I ring Dad? He can tell us what to do.

Caroline: That's a very good idea, Emma. Tell him to ring the police. We need to get out of this mess.

15 **Emma:** Oh no! I haven't got any signal! Caroline, Rajiv, you try it.

They all get out their phones, but none of them has got signal.

Caroline: I haven't got any.

Rajiv: This seems to be a dead spot.

---

4 to turn on/off /ˌtɜːn ˈɒn, ˌtɜːn ˈɒf/ – *an-/ausschalten* **17** none /nʌn/ – *keine(r)* **19** dead spot /ˌded ˈspɒt/ – *Funkloch*

Emma: Oh no!

Suddenly there is a loud noise offstage.

Gillian: Listen! I think it's our men in black. Put your phones away, quick!

5 **Charlie:** *(speaks like a ghost)* Argh, Sir Percival!

George: Oh, shut up, Charlie.

George turns off his torch.

31

Tom and Dave come into the room carrying torches and sacks. It is dark but you can see their torches. They look for the children with their torches, but they don't find them. Dave is very nervous.

5   **Narrator:** The thieves come back into the Great Hall. They don't know where the children are, but now they are only interested in the silver.

Tom: Right, now it's time to take the expensive things. Put those silver things in your sack, Dave.

10   **Dave:** *(nervous)* OK Tom, then let's get out of here quick. I think I can hear something. Perhaps it's that ghost …

Tom: Don't be silly, Dave. There is no ghost. We have to get the jewellery from the next room first. Come on, I've got a hammer for the glass.

15   *They leave.*

Caroline: *(very worried)* What do we do now, George? We can't phone the police, we haven't got signal.

George: Then we must catch the thieves and tie them up first. After that we can go outside and phone. Look, I've got 20   an idea. Charlie, we need your ghost. Take the cape and the helmet from the suit of armour and come with me. The rest of you take the tablecloth and wait at the door. You can catch them with it and then tie them up.

Caught in the act – *Auf frischer Tat ertappt* **1** to carry /ˈkæri/ – *tragen* **18** to tie (up) /ˌtaɪˈʌp/ – *fesseln* **20** cape /keɪp/ – *Umhang* **21** helmet /ˈhelmɪt/ – *Helm*

Charlie puts on the helmet and the cape and leaves with George. Caroline and Emma take the tablecloth off the table.

Rajiv: But what can we use to tie them up?

Gillian: I've got a scarf and what about Emma's belt?

5 **Emma:** No way!

Caroline: Emma – this is important.

Emma: Oh, all right – but you must give it back to me later.

She gives it to Rajiv. Suddenly they hear a scream and the sound of glass from the next room.

---

2 to take off /ˌteɪk ˈɒf/ – *abnehmen* **4** belt /belt/ – *Gürtel*

Rajiv: Come on everybody, over here.

Caroline and Emma hold the tablecloth in front of the door.
The two thieves run into the tablecloth. Caroline and Emma
wrap the tablecloth around the thieves. Rajiv and Gillian tie
5 *their feet together. George and Charlie come back, too. Charlie*
is still wearing the helmet and the cape.

Charlie: *(speaks like a ghost)* You mustn't steal from Sir
Percival Caxton! You horrible creature, you!

Dave: *(very nervous)* I'm sorry, Sir Percival. You can have it all
10 back. Please, just let me go.

Tom: Oh, shut up, Dave. I'm sure it's not a real ghost, it's those
children.

Rajiv and Gillian sit the two men down. They are in the
middle of the stage. The children shine their torches in their
15 *faces. Just then they hear some people talking and then*
somebody turns the lights on.

Guard 4: *(angry)* Come this way! I'm sure this is where those
horrible children are hiding. Who knows what they
are doing – there's probably rubbish everywhere, and
20 graffiti on the doors. Somebody must pay for all this.

The guard and two policemen come onto the stage. They are
very surprised to see the scene in front of them.
The two thieves are on two chairs. The children are watching
them.

---

4 to wrap around /ræp_əˈraʊnd/ – *einwickeln* **14** to shine /ʃaɪn/ – *anstrahlen*
21 policeman (*pl* policemen) /pəˈliːsmən/ – *Polizist*

Policeman 1, Bill: Right, what's going on? What are you kids doing here after closing time? You should be home with …!

Policeman 2, Harry: What a surprise. The terrible twins, Tom and Dave.

5 **Policeman 1, Bill:** Just out of prison and back in prison again soon.

Tom: No, it's not us. Those kids are the thieves. Look, they've got all the stuff. We are just visiting the castle.

George: Ha, ha. That's a good trick, but don't worry, your
10 fingerprints are on the silver.

---

3 terrible /ˈterəb(ə)l/ – *schrecklich* **8** stuff *(informal)* /stʌf/ – *Zeug*
10 fingerprint /ˈfɪŋɡə(r)ˌprɪnt/ – *Fingerabdruck*

Emma: Please, Sir. They are the thieves, not us. You must believe us.

Policeman 2, Harry: And why are you children all here?

Gillian: Well, that's quite a long story.

5   **Policeman 1, Bill:** And I've got lots of time to listen to it. *(to his colleague)* Harry, take Tom and Dave to the police station.

Policeman 2, Harry: Right, Bill! *(to Tom and Dave)* Come on, you two.

10   *He takes them out.*

Dave: *(very unhappy)* But I don't want to go to prison. But I don't want to …

Policeman 1, Bill: Right, now you can tell me all about it. Who wants to start?

15   *The children all start talking at once.*

---

6 colleague /ˈkɒliːɡ/ – *Kollege* **10** to take out /ˌteɪkˈaʊt/ – *hinausbringen*

Tasks

Scene 1

1 What do the children want?

a) Match the children to the things they want on their day out.
There is one more thing than you need.

1 Emma   **A** football

2 Caroline   **B** a ghost

3 Gillian   **C** a picnic

4 George and Rajiv   **D** the castle

5 Charlie   **E** an audio guide tour

                         F jousting and knights

b) Now write the sentences. Use the verbs *to have* or *to see*.

1 Emma *wants to have an audio guide tour.* _____

2 Caroline _____.

3 Gillian _____.

4 George and Rajiv _____.

5 Charlie _____.

2 Adjectives

Use the right adjectives from the box to complete the sentences.

interesting • boring • exciting • delicious • real • fun • true • famous

1 Caroline loves _____ picnics.

2 Gillian likes castles because they are _____.

3 George thinks history is _____.

4 George doesn't want to look at _____ pictures.

5 Caroline says that Charlie's story about the ghost isn't

_____.

6 Charlie reads about ghosts on the website. He thinks they are very

_____.

7 Emma thinks the story about the murderer is _____.

8 Rajiv doesn't want to watch the jousting. He wants to be a

_____ knight.

3 Sir Percival Caxton

Draw a picture of the ghost of Sir Percival and
write a short text about him.
These questions can help you:

- What do you know about him?
- When does he come out at night?
- Why can't he sleep?
- Where does he hide in the castle?
- What does he look like?

You can use your own ideas, too.

Scene 2

1 Find the mistakes

Read this summary of scene 2 and underline the ten mistakes.
Can you correct them? Write the correct words below.

When the children come to the castle, they
see some tents. Gillian thinks the <u>cakes</u> look
delicious but they decide to eat their picnic
first. George isn't hungry and wants to watch
the football. Charlie goes with him. Caroline
has got some fruit in her picnic but she likes
Emma's chicken nuggets. Gillian suddenly
sees two men behind a tent. They are wearing
blue clothes and one of them has got a mask.

The two men are planning to steal some
money from the castle. Then they want to go
to Africa. Dave is very happy. He doesn't want
to go to prison again. Tom tells him that he
has got a silly plan and Dave needn't worry.
The children decide to stop the thieves and
talk to the police.

1 _hot dogs_

2 _____

3 _____

4 _____

5 _____

6 _____

7 _____

8 _____

9 _____

10 _____

2 A picnic on a day out

What can you eat and drink on a picnic? Circle ten things.

E	L	E	M	O	N	A	D	E	T	C	A	K	I
C	H	O	C	O	L	A	T	E	H	A	O	L	P
J	L	E	I	F	R	U	I	T	L	K	P	W	P
U	G	R	C	K	E	Z	S	C	I	E	N	H	L
I	E	Y	E	M	O	N	A	H	S	O	I	O	F
C	H	I	C	K	E	N	N	U	G	G	E	T	S
E	I	W	R	N	N	U	D	G	R	O	V	D	L
F	N	U	E	O	U	T	W	S	H	R	O	O	N
R	Y	Q	A	A	S	E	I	W	M	T	H	G	A
O	T	E	M	T	H	A	C	U	E	E	L	S	D
A	H	L	D	P	L	M	H	R	O	N	Y	T	S
M	A	P	P	L	E	S	E	F	R	U	K	L	Y
N	B	B	O	U	Y	W	S	A	P	P	W	V	I

3 A day at Caxton Castle

Design a poster about Caxton Castle.

- Write a short text about the castle.
- You can write down when the castle opens and closes.
- Note down what you can do at the castle.
- You can draw a picture of the castle.
- You can use your own ideas, too.

Scene 3

1 **The guards**

What happens in scene 3?
Match the sentence halves and
write five sentences.

1 First the children can't speak

2 The children are very excited

3 But the guards are angry

4 The guards don't believe the children

5 So the children decide to go

A because they think the story about the thieves isn't true.

B because they are out of breath.

C because they need a new plan.

D because they want to tell the guards about the thieves.

E because they are having their tea break.

2 Say it in English

Find the phrases in scene 3 and write them down.

Was sagst du, wenn jemand …

1 sich beeilen soll? _____

2 sich beruhigen soll? _____

3 zurückkommen soll? _____

4 nicht mehr reden soll? _____

5 leise sein soll? _____

6 zuhören soll? _____

3 Bert and Sid

After the children go, the guards Bert and Sid talk about them.
Write a short dialogue between them.

Scene 4

1 George's plan

Tick ✔ the correct answer.

1 When the friends come,
George wants to …
- [ ] a) talk about the tournament.
- [ ] b) go home.
- [ ] c) have some lunch.

2 When the friends tell him
about the thieves, George …
- [ ] a) doesn't believe them.
- [ ] b) has a plan to catch them.
- [ ] c) goes back to the guards.

3 Emma and Caroline think
George's plan is …
- [ ] a) dangerous.
- [ ] b) silly.
- [ ] c) exciting.

4 Gillian and Charlie think
George's plan is …
- [ ] a) boring.
- [ ] b) bad.
- [ ] c) fun.

5 In the end the children decide
to …
- [ ] a) phone their parents.
- [ ] b) follow the men.
- [ ] c) tell the police.

2 Who is it?

Write down the correct word. What do we call people who …

1 steal things? _____

2 fight in tournaments? _____

3 watch a play or a film? _____

4 try to catch thieves? _____

5 watch people in a castle or a museum? _____

6 have children? _____

3   Wanted poster

Write down the information
about the thieves.
You can look at the example
for help.

wanted – *gesucht*

WANTED

Name: Greg

Description: black jumper

Job: thief

Character: very angry, not clever

WANTED

Name: _____   _____

Description: _____   _____

_____   _____

Job: _____   _____

Character: _____   _____

_____   _____

Scene 5

🟦 1 In the Great Hall

Put the sentences in the right order.
Look at pages 22-26 for help.

A Dave and Tom come into the Great Hall.

B The children say they are looking at a picture of Sir Percival.

C Dave is very nervous because he thinks the children know about them.

D When Tom and Dave hear voices, they hide under a table.

E Tom tells Dave to shut up and to follow him.

F Rajiv, Emma and Caroline don't know where the thieves are.

G The unfriendly guard pushes the children to the door.

H An unfriendly guard tells the children to move on to the next room.

1	2	3	4	5	6	7	8
A							

2 Look at, look for, look like, …?

Complete the sentences with the right form of *look* from the box.

> *look like · look for · look at · look · look around*

1 The children want to know if the guard is following them so they

_____.

2 The six friends want to _____ Tom and Dave in the castle.

3 The guard doesn't _____ very friendly.

4 Caroline _____ the picture of Sir Percival.

5 Rajiv thinks the picture _____ Sir Percival.

3 Tom and Dave

a) Who says it? Draw lines from the speech bubbles to Tom or Dave.
Then write their dialogue.

1 Don't worry! I know what I'm doing.

2 I've got this funny feeling.

3 They're just some silly kids looking for an adventure.

4 Something is wrong with your plan.

5 My ear itches. Believe me, it's a bad sign.

6 That's nothing to worry about.

Tom

Dave

b) What do you think they say after they leave the Great Hall? Write
two more sentences for each of them.

47

Scene 6

1 Right or wrong?

a) Are the sentences about scene 6 right or wrong? Tick ✔ right or wrong.

		right	wrong
→	The children look for the thieves everywhere.		✔
1	They decide to hide in the castle.		
2	Charlie hopes that he can see the ghost.		
3	Gillian gives the guard her mobile phone.		
4	Emma is excited about George's plan.		
5	When the castle closes, the children are hiding under the table.		
6	Emma rings her father and talks to him about their problem.		

b) Correct the wrong sentences.

→ *The children can't look everywhere.*

48

2 Verb snakes

a) Find verbs from scene 6 in the snakes and write them down.

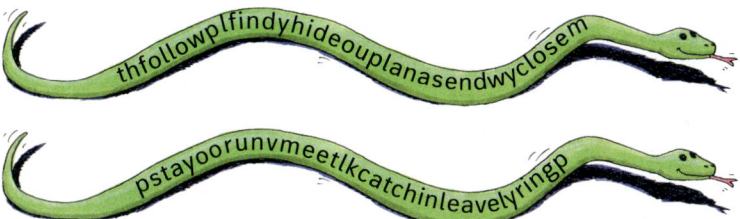

b) Use some of the verbs to finish the sentences.

1 The guard _____ the children all the time.

2 George's group want to _____ in the castle at night.

3 Gillian decides to _____ the other group a text message.

4 Emma doesn't want to _____ in the castle.

5 Gillian: "We have only got this chance to _____ the thieves."

6 They children can't _____ their parents because they haven't got signal.

c) Write three more sentences with the other verbs from the snakes.

3 A good plan?

Talk to a partner. What do you think about George's plan?
These phrases can help you:

I think George's plan is good/bad/dangerous/clever/silly because …
It's a good/bad idea to … because …
I think the plan may go wrong because …
I don't believe/believe the children can catch the thieves because …

Scene 7

1 Caught in the act

Answer the questions about scene 7 in a few words.

1 What things do Tom and Dave want to steal?

_____

2 Why do the children need the tablecloth?

_____

3 What do the children use to tie up the thieves?

_____

4 What is the policemen's name for Tom and Dave?

_____

5 How can the police know that the children are not the thieves?

_____

6 Where does Harry go with Tom and Dave?

_____

2 A crossword

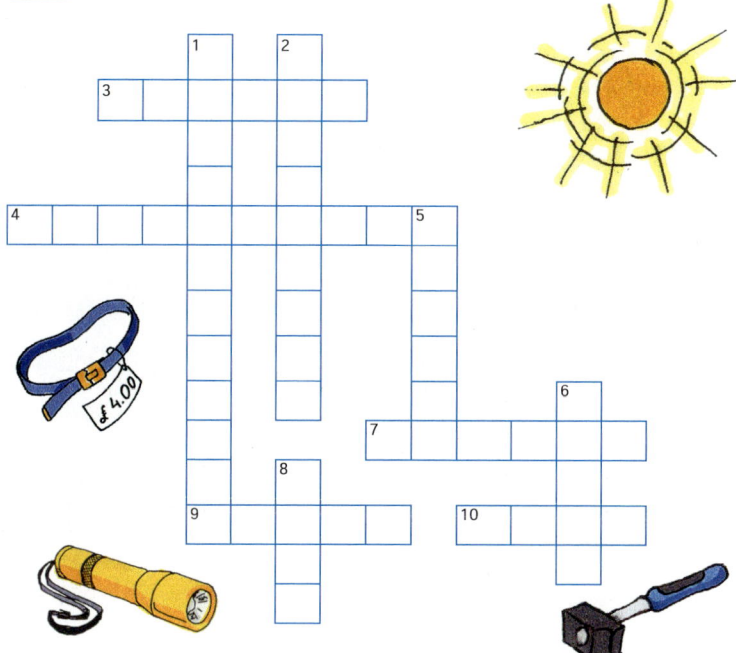

Across →

3 In summer the sun _____ and keeps us warm.

4 You can put this on a table. It is often white.

7 When the police catch thieves, they send them here.

9 Take something away and not ask or pay for it.

10 You can put things in it. It is like a very big bag.

Down ↓

1 Thieves leave these if they don't wear gloves.

2 Expensive gold and silver things. You can wear them.

5 You can use this to break glass.

6 It gives you light.

8 You wear this to keep your jeans up.

3 The policeman

What do you think the policeman says to the children after he hears their story? Write down his words. These questions can help you:

- Is he angry with them?
- Does he think they are clever?
- What must they do next time?
- Does he want to talk to their parents?

Extra

A text about the play

Write a text about the play for someone who doesn't know it. Write about the story and the characters. The questions can help you.

Story:
- What happens in the play?
- Do you like the story?
- What is funny/scary/interesting/boring?
- What do you think about the ending?

Characters:
- Who do you like/don't you like? Say why.
- Who do you want to be in the play? Say why.

Solutions

Scene 1

1 What do the children want?
a) 1 E | 2 C | 3 D | 4 F | 5 B
b) 2 Caroline wants to have a picnic. | 3 Gillian wants to see the castle. | 4 George and Rajiv want to see jousting and knights. | 5 Charlie wants to see a ghost.

2 Adjectives
1 delicious | 2 fun | 3 boring | 4 famous | 5 true | 6 interesting | 7 exciting | 8 real

3 Sir Percival Caxton
Individuelle Lösung

Scene 2

1 Find the mistakes
1 hot dogs | 2 jousting | 3 (cheese) sandwiches | 4 Rajiv | 5 black | 6 silver and jewellery | 7 America | 8 nervous | 9 clever | 10 guard

2 A picnic on a day out

E	L	E	M	O	N	A	D	E	T	C	A	K	I
C	H	O	C	O	I	A	T	E	H	A	O	L	P
J	L	E	I	F	R	U	I	T	L	K	P	W	P
U	G	R	C	K	E	Z	S	C	I	E	N	H	L
I	E	Y	E	M	O	N	A	H	S	O	I	O	F
C	H	I	C	K	E	N	N	U	G	G	E	T	S
E	I	W	R	N	N	U	D	G	R	O	V	D	L
F	N	U	E	O	U	T	W	S	H	R	O	O	N
R	Y	Q	A	A	S	E	I	W	M	T	H	G	A
O	T	E	M	T	H	A	C	U	E	E	L	S	D
A	H	L	D	P	L	M	H	R	O	N	Y	T	S
M	A	P	P	L	E	S	E	F	R	U	K	L	Y
N	B	B	O	U	Y	W	S	A	P	P	W	V	I

3 A day at Caxton Castle
Individuelle Lösung

Scene 3

1 The guards
1   First the children can't speak because they are out of breath.
2   The children are very excited because they want to tell the guards about the thieves.
3   But the guards are angry because they are having their tea break.
4   The guards don't believe the children because they think the story about the thieves isn't true.
5   So the children decide to go because they need a new plan.

2 Say it in English
1 Hurry up! | 2 Calm down! | 3 Come back! | 4 Stop talking! |
5 Don't make a noise! | 6 Listen!

3 Bert and Sid
Individuelle Lösung

Scene 4

1 George's plan
1 c) | 2 b) | 3 a) | 4 c) | 5 b)

2 Who is it?
1 thieves | 2 knights | 3 audience | 4 detectives/police |
5 guards | 6 parents

3 Wanted poster

Name:	Tom	Dave
Job:	thief	thief
Description:	black clothes, sack under jumper	black clothes, mask
Character:	silly, not dangerous, thinks he is clever	silly, not dangerous, nervous, makes mistakes

Scene 5

1 In the Great Hall
1 A | **2** D | **3** F | **4** H | **5** B | **6** G | **7** C | **8** E

2 Look at, look for, look like, …?
1 look around | **2** look for | **3** look | **4** looks at | **5** looks like

3 Tom and Dave
a) **1** Tom | **2** Dave | **3** Tom | **4** Dave | **5** Dave | **6** Tom

Dave: I've got this funny feeling. Something is wrong with your plan. My ear itches. Believe me, it's a bad sign.

Tom:　Don't worry! I know what I'm doing. They're just some silly kids looking for an adventure. That's nothing to worry about.

b) Individuelle Lösung

Scene 6

1 Right or wrong?
a) **1** right | **2** right | **3** wrong | **4** wrong | **5** right | **6** wrong

b) **3** Gillian doesn't give the guard her mobile phone. **4** Emma isn't excited about George's plan. **6** Emma can't ring her father.

2 Verb snakes

a) follow | find | hide | plan | send | close | stay | run | meet | catch | leave | ring

b) **1** follows | **2** hide | **3** send | **4** stay | **5** catch | **6** ring

c) Individuelle Lösung

3 A good plan?

Individuelle Lösung

Scene 7

1 Caught in the act

1 silver and jewellery | **2** to catch the thieves | **3** Emma's belt and Gillian's scarf | **4** the terrible twins | **5** the thieves' fingerprints are on the silver | **6** to the police station

2 A crossword

Down: 1 fingerprints | **2** jewellery | **5** hammer | **6** torch | **8** belt

Across: 3 shines | **4** tablecloth | **7** prison | **9** steal | **10** sack

3 The policeman

Individuelle Lösung

Extra

A text about the play

Individuelle Lösung